True **Mom** Confessions

True **Mom** Confessions

Real Moms Get Real

Romi Lassally and the mothers of
truemomconfessions.com

BERKLEY BOOKS, NEW YORK

THE BERKLEY PUBLISHING GROUP
Published by the Penguin Group
Penguin Group (USA) Inc.
375 Hudson Street, New York, New York 10014, USA
Penguin Group (Canada), 90 Eglinton Avenue East, Suite 700, Toronto, Ontario M4P 2Y3,
Canada (a division of Pearson Penguin Canada Inc.)
Penguin Books Ltd., 80 Strand, London WC2R 0RL, England
Penguin Group Ireland, 25 St. Stephen's Green, Dublin 2, Ireland
(a division of Penguin Books Ltd.)
Penguin Group (Australia), 250 Camberwell Road, Camberwell, Victoria 3124, Australia
(a division of Pearson Australia Group Pty. Ltd.)
Penguin Books India Pvt. Ltd., 11 Community Centre, Panchsheel Park, New Delhi—110 017,
India
Penguin Group (NZ), 67 Apollo Drive, Rosedale, North Shore, 0632, New Zealand
(a division of Pearson New Zealand Ltd.)
Penguin Books (South Africa) (Pty.) Ltd., 24 Sturdee Avenue, Rosebank, Johannesburg 2196,
South Africa

Penguin Books Ltd., Registered Offices: 80 Strand, London WC2R 0RL, England

The publisher does not have any control over and does not assume any responsibility for author
or third-party websites or their content.

PRINTING HISTORY
Berkley trade paperback edition / April 2009

Library of Congress Cataloging-in-Publication Data

Lassally, Romi.
    True mom confessions : real moms get real / Romi Lassally and the mothers of
truemomconfessions.com.
        p. cm.
    ISBN 978-0-425-22604-9
    1. Mothers—Miscellanea.   2. Motherhood—Miscellanea.   I. Title.

    HQ759.L3724   2009
    306.874'3—dc22

                                                            2008047667

To the three who call me mommy, momma, and *moooommmm!* Phoebe, Annabel and Owen

ACKNOWLEDGMENTS

True Mom Confessions—the book and the website—would not have come into being were it not for a fateful phone call with Cooper Munroe of themotherhood.com in which I confessed to a shameful mom moment and was inspired to create a place for other mothers to do the same. It wouldn't have happened without Katie, Tucker and Rebecca who aren't on the rollercoaster with me anymore, but who were great partners in the beginning. It wouldn't have happened without those who are still hanging on—Lauren and Jill and especially Maegan, who despite her fear of poop and vomit, remains steadfast in the trenches with us every day. And a special thank-you to Ralph—who like a mother—has invested so much time and energy without much visible reward.

Rachel Fershleiser deserves a big shout out for her expert editorial help and uncanny ability to sift through hundreds of thousands of tiny entries, and create a semblance of order. When I could no longer see the forest (or in this case the confessions) for the trees, she always had clear and keen vision.

I am so grateful to all the writers and bloggers who succumbed to my e-mail nagging and wrote the wonderful Confessays sprinkled throughout the book. Each of them contributed their unique and intimate experiences as mothers—some sharing details never before revealed, certainly not in their day jobs.

True Mom Confessions would have remained in cyberspace alone were it not for the diligent web surfing of my editor, Denise Silvestro, who thankfully saw the humor and pathos in the online mommy confessional and took a flyer. The writing of the book nicely dovetailed with the pregnancy and birth of her second child, so the way I see it—while she had one baby, I was fortunate enough to be the surrogate for another.

Thanks to my mom for her endless devotion and encouragement. If there ever was a tireless cheerleader with a constant, "You go girl!"—it is her. Thanks to my gaggle of children—Phoebe, Annabel and Owen—who didn't complain too much about my shoddy mothering while

I neglected them to read about other mothers' guilt over neglecting their own kids. And last but certainly not least, thank you to my adoring husband, Tom, who over the past year spent many a night next to a warm laptop instead of a warm body. Honey, I owe you.

ACKNOWLEDGMENTS

CONTENTS

CONTENTS

FOREWORD

by Gail Saltz, M.D.

Being a mother is one of the most difficult jobs in the world. It holds the promise of unmatched joy yet unparalleled pain. Most mothers have an ideal of what they want to be as a parent. This ideal arises from a combination of who their mother was, what they feel about that relationship, what the culture around them defines as good mothering, and their own inner voice about being the "right" kind of mother. From the many women I have seen and talked with about being a mom—and the entries in this book—I would say more often than not their ideal is nothing less than *perfectionistic*.

Most women, consciously or not, do not make room for being a human being. There is no place in their mother-child dyad for being angry, frustrated, bored, sad, conflicted about the burden, or even regretful. But the fact is that all these feelings are normal parts of being a mother. Most women who realize they have negative feelings find themselves guilt-ridden, ashamed and are even self-destructive in order to mete out the punishment they feel they deserve. And so they keep their feelings a secret—not only from others but also from themselves.

What happens with a burning secret? Secrets of wishes to escape, get out from under, be far less than your best, be unfair, harsh or hurtful, betray, have someone else take care of you? Most often they take the form of fantasy. You daydream about running away, having a fight, being on an island, having sex with someone else, doing that crazy thing with no restraints. But conscious fantasy is a healthy expression for wishes and dreams you likely will never act upon. They allow a little relief while not having you actually do the thing that might hurt someone else or make you feel really bad.

However, when these secret feelings are so shameful that you can't even bear to let yourself know they are there, they may come out in the form of an intrusive thought that invades your mind when you least want it to and leaves you shaken and guilty. Many women have thoughts of leaving their child by the roadside and taking off. They will never do such a thing but they are tormented by the unwanted vision. It frightens them because they do not understand that such thoughts are often the expression of an unconscious ambivalence about being a mother, which is really very normal. As long as such thoughts remain unconscious, unexplained and a secret, they will continue to have the power to produce seemingly mysterious thoughts that shame and torture.

This is why sharing a secret can be so relieving, healing, and reparative. And that is why True Mom Confessions is such a valuable platform for women. In order to share a secret with another, you must first reveal it to yourself. Making something conscious and being able to mull it over allows you to analyze yourself and gain both understanding and comfort from others. For some mothers, the simple act of acknowledging their secret thoughts is enough to help them be less judgmental about themselves. For others, revealing these truths to someone else can be even more relieving because sharing a secret creates intimacy and makes one feel less alone. It often serves as a testing ground, giving moms the opportunity to ask, "Will they judge me? If they still think I am OK, does that mean I can forgive myself, too?"

What I know from my practice and personal experience is that most women are more afraid of being judged by their peers than anyone else. That is why a forum like TrueMom Confessions.com and this book are so important. It takes judgment out of the equation and offers a safe, anonymous place for sharing, acknowledging and weighing our own thoughts. It gives women a place to tell their truths, read the personal stories of others in similar situations and come away realizing that we all have maternal ambivalence at times. It allows women to acknowledge, and even rejoice in the knowledge, that they are not crazy, not alone, not a "bad mother." I'm hopeful that this book will encourage more mothers to be honest with themselves and with others. Only then will these secrets no longer have the power to hurt us or rob us of the intense pleasure that can be found in mothering.

True **Mom**
Confessions

"I was hoping the dog would eat it."

Last March, my six-year-old son, Owen, stumbled out of his bedroom and vomited all over himself and the hallway carpet. He cried for help and I dashed downstairs—maternal sensors on high alert. When I reached him, as if on cue, he proceeded to throw up all over me. Now I'm no stranger to middle-of-the-night barfing, but I must admit that even after fifteen years of mothering, I wretch at the sight and smell of it and I've never, ever mastered cleaning it up. To avoid all of the above, I whisked my little man away from the scene of the crime, sponged him off as best I could and took us both up to my bed. What of the throw up you might ask? I left it there in all its steamy, goopy glory. I was hoping the dog would eat it.

Later that week I recounted the story of my parental/ housekeeping "DON'T" to a girlfriend who winced in disgust but also gave me kudos for my ingenuity. Turns out every mother can appreciate a shortcut now and then. She then blurted out her own mommy misdemeanor, something she'd been mortified to admit to anyone: recently on a long plane flight, she'd dosed her three-year-old with Benadryl to get her to fall sleep.

"Am I awful to have drugged her for a few hours of peace at thirty-five thousand feet?"

Our shared secrets and support of each other opened the floodgates and we sat there baring our conflicted, guilt-ridden and shame-filled souls. I followed the vomit story with my most recent transgression—reading my teenager's IM chats—and she offered up another burning secret: she was thinking of leaving her job but didn't know if she had the stomach or the bank account to be a stay-at-home mom. Ah, the truth.

What I recognized from this exchange (but really had known in my gut for most of my life as a mom) was that the mere act of confessing to a less-than-perfect motherly moment provided quick and much-needed relief, with the added bonus of prompting another mother to tell her own tales from the trenches. So why not figure out a way for more mothers to do this all the time? Wouldn't we all be better for it?

Being realistic, I acknowledged that most women didn't have the confessional gene that I did; that the fear of judgment, criticism, or worse—rejection—might keep them from sharing the gritty details of their lives face-to-face. And even if they did, the frenetic lives of mothers don't always offer up the time, place or the *Sex in the City*–type girlfriends ready to lend an ear (or a cocktail) when we moms need it the most. But online, under the veil of anonymity and with 24/7 accessibility, I believed the conversation about the REAL not the IDEAL of motherhood could flourish.

So TrueMomConfessions.com was born. Finally, an outlet for women to spill their secrets: what they did (and didn't do) and what they thought about but were afraid to talk about during their daily trials and triumphs as mothers.

The experiment was a rousing success, with women coming from across the globe to "confess themselves" and to revel in the heartfelt and hilarious admissions of others. Being honest makes us stronger mothers and sharing our stories helps us learn from one another. It's just that simple. It has been so satisfying to see that a website encouraging candor could spark so many conversations and build

3

a community of unabashedly frank women all doing their best, making a mess and finding a lot of reasons to laugh (and cry) along the way.

So why publish a book? Because we all live hectic, harried lives and logging on isn't always an option. I thought I could take the wisest and most liberating of the confessions and put them in a portable package to be snacked on anytime, anywhere. These pages are clustered around themes that emerged from hundreds of thousands of bite-sized entries. So whether you've got five minutes stuck in traffic or an hour in the tub, you can open a chapter and find shared experiences, diverse perspectives, or some simple solution you hadn't thought of before.

I hope this book provides solace, guidance and a healthy dose of humor. Above all, I hope it's good company—honest and authentic voices that paint a portrait of motherhood today—to remind you that we are all struggling with the idea that being a "good" mother means being good enough.

P.S. The dog did eat the throw up but then threw up himself. *That* I did clean up myself.

A NOTE ON TERMINOLOGY

Along with unique opportunities to argue, connect and vent without fear of retribution, the blogosphere relies on some unique abbreviations to reference the folks we love and loathe. This book talks about:

DH   Dear Husband. Except when it means Dull Husband, Dumbass Husband, or Dickhead.

DS and DD   Dear Son and Dear Daughter. Occasionally, but less frequently, modified as per above.

MiL   Mother-in-Law. Imagine your own less flattering permutations.

And then there's:

STFU   Shut the f&*k up. Self-explanatory.

SAHM   Stay-at-Home Mom. Familial ideal or feminist betrayal. Discuss.

WAHM   Work-at-Home Mom. Writers, bloggers, and freelancers of all stripes often juggle it all from the comfort of home.

Little White Lies

"I told my son the cops would come."

When my daughter Annabel was five years old, she piped up from her car seat, "What's the 'f' word?"

Although no prude, I wasn't ready to deliver that information, nor the meaning of the act or the mysteries and intricacies of love and sex. So I blurted out, "Well honey, it means 'fart off.'"

To my surprise this morsel of misinformation appeased her. It must have sounded logical because technically "fart" is an "f" word. But I immediately regretted this because I knew the truth would get out at some point. And rightly so.

Days later, Annabel was thrown in with a pack of girls several years her senior and worldly wise beyond that. Information is power—especially to the under five-foot set—so in an attempt to find equal footing, my little girl offered up her very grown-up information.

Needless to say, her words were met with snickering. A moment later, she was charging at me, breaking through the wall of mothers I was talking to, and demanding an explanation. I was mortified. I stammered and apologized and told her that I had no good excuse for telling her the wrong word, and such a silly one at that. I took her aside and whispered the real one—I spelled it out actually—still not ready to utter such a harsh expletive in the presence of freckles, innocence and youth.

She looked at me with a "Really?" expression and I shook my head and apologized again for misleading her. "That's OK, mommy," she said, "but you really shouldn't tell lies."

Ouch.

One of the many sordid secrets of parenting is that the job involves telling little white lies and half-truths. The books don't tell you this, and frankly, your friends don't tell you this because to do so would be admitting their own guilt.

From the pages ahead you'll see that moms everywhere are contributing to the grand conspiracy and fib to their progeny for a host of reasons—to bribe and cajole them, to put an end to a never-ending story, or to scare the bejeesus out of them so they will finally just GO. TO. SLEEP.

It's ironic that with a mission to help women tell the truth, here I am promoting just the opposite. But therein lies one of the many paradoxes of parenting: sometimes what we tout as a sin to our kids is, in a moment of weakness, what we need to do to save our sanity.

My son knows he's not allowed downstairs until 9 AM. He wakes up, calls down to let me know he's awake, goes potty and then climbs back in bed with a few toys. Reason why? He's been told that between 8 AM and 9 AM, Mommy's fighting the monster that lives in the laundry basket.

I am taking Friday off work as a "personal day." My boss thinks I have an appointment with an attorney. So far, the plan is to drop my son off at preschool, then I have a 9:30 AM at the spa, 1 PM highlights at the salon, and then I am coming home to relax until 5 PM when I normally pick him up! Three years of being a single working mom, I think I DESERVE this!!! I am so excited I can't wait!!

It's been one of *those* days. I just ate a full pint of Häagen-Dazs, and when my three-year-old asked me what I was eating, I told her it was special medicine for mommies because I didn't want to share.

I told my son the cops would come "have a talk with him" if he didn't stop ripping my eardrums apart with his tantrum screams.

My children have the day off from school on Thursday. I requested the day off from work because my babysitter was not available, but she rearranged her schedule and is able to watch the kids. I am thinking of going to the beach alone. I will pretend I am going off to work. Either that or I will tell the sitter to unlock my bedroom slider doors so I can sneak in and stay in bed all day and read without the kids knowing. Is that so wrong?

I lie to my friends about how much I let my kid play on the computer.

I hide the extra helmet so I have an excuse not to wear one when my kids and I go for bike rides.

I took sixty dollars from my son's piggy bank—and when he realized it was empty I blamed it on his sister.

"No, honey. I would never read your diary. Or your e-mail. Or the IM chats you leave up on the screen." But of course I do.

The goldfish didn't die of "natural causes" like I told the kids. I forgot to feed them.

I told my nine-year-old daughter there was no Easter Bunny. She quickly put the pieces together that no Bunny meant no Tooth Fairy and no Santa. She cried for an entire week, asking me how she could live in a world with no magic. I wish I had never told her the truth . . .

All my friends on my parenting message board think I am happily married. I have never been married.

I just found out a week ago that I have breast cancer. I have not told anyone. Not even my husband. And I don't think I will be able to let my kids know.

I hate one of my daughter's favorite shirts ... so last night I painted it with red nail polish and told her that it was ruined beyond repair.

I almost didn't go to my son's award ceremony yesterday. I was going to tell him that I was there and that he just didn't see me. Then I remember all the times my mom did that to me and how much I hated her for not telling the truth. I ended up going and I was glad. I never want to be as poor a mother as my mom was.

I live in a small apartment complex and am friends with most of the other moms. We hang out on the playground and chat every day. None of them know that my husband moved out two weeks ago because he decided to come out of the closet. I'm too ashamed to tell them that I'm living by myself now.

My son was so excited for his second birthday, but when the day rolled around I hadn't pulled anything together to celebrate—so I told him that he had the day wrong and his birthday was actually the following week. (Yes . . . he believed me and I felt terrible!)

LITTLE WHITE LIES

Today, when I saw my neighbor seven months pregnant and with three kids around her ankles, I told myself I'd be in the loony bin, but the truth is, I wish more than anything I was her.

Both DD and I were sick earlier this week and DH took care of us. But even though I felt much better today, I still said "not so good" when he asked how I felt so I could get a day of "me time" away from both of them. I feel guilty, but rested for the first time in forever.

I had an Irish coffee for breakfast this morning. Okay I lied. I had two Irish coffees for breakfast this morning and another one right now for nap time. I'll probably have a fourth with DH after the kids are in bed.

I never thought I'd say . . .

**"Don't pee on your brother
in the living room."**

"We don't lick bricks, honey."

"I'll help you walk on the ceiling
after I finish the dishes."

"Stop pulling your brother's penis."

"One day you'll LIKE having testicles."

True Mom Poll
What would you never admit to your kids?

How young you were when you first had sex: 18%

What drugs you took and when: 8%

How often you skipped class: 8%

That you drove drunk . . . often: 7%

That you broke the law
(you know, shoplifted or something like that): 7%

All of the above: 26%

None of the above: 6%

"We can't keep houseplants alive."

(or Riding the Short Bus to Redemption)

by Kyran Pittman

This morning I remembered that tomorrow is Pinewood Derby day for my son, our resident Cub Scout. This means we should have already built a wooden car to Scout specifications, and clearly we have not. When I brought it up with my husband, it was obvious that my earlier reminders had somehow slipped beneath the radar. In the interest of preserving the marital trust, I will now enable the mute button on the scene that followed. But if you were to write captions based on observing our body language and facial expressions, you might come up with something like this:

Me: "Are you f*&king crazy??"

Him: "Are you??"

And that would more or less capture the gist of it.

I would love to tell you that we are a couple that always meets adversity with a unified front. Grace under pressure. But the truth is, when things go awry, we sometimes turn on, and not toward, each other. Certain situations trigger our own insecurities, rip open old wounds. The defenses go up and the pointing fingers come out. This was one of those situations.

Sometimes—most times—I think we are doing a pretty good job as parents. I have been known to joke that our kids won the baby lottery when they pulled our number. They slept between us as infants. They were breastfed into toddlerhood. They never had to cry longer than it took us to figure out what was needed and answer the need. We may not always keep up with the Joneses, but they have bikes, books and bunk beds, soccer, school and Scouts, and most of the other privileges of being a middle-class kid in America. We work hard at being whole people in a healthy relationship. Most times, I think my kids are as lucky to have us as we are to have them.

But then we hit a bump like today and it derails me completely. Instead of feeling like we are doing an outstanding job, I wonder who thought it would be a good idea to give us three human beings to care for. We can't keep houseplants alive. We can't change lightbulbs. We can't sew badges on uniforms. Hell, we can't remember to wash the uniform, let alone remember the Pinewood

Derby Cub Scout car races. I know people of lower intellectual capacity who seem to have no problem at all with going to work, paying their bills, mowing their lawns, dusting their ceiling fans, painting the door frames and returning their library books on time. What is wrong with us? I ask myself on days like this. Did we miss an orientation session on Living Life? Did we ride in on the short bus?

Procrastination is a character trait that has pained me all my life, the one that I would spare my children from if I could. The other night it was my first turn at leading my son's Scout den, a duty I had agreed to take over from the other leaders at the turn of the year. I still don't have my leader uniform. I read the meeting literature in my office over lunch. I scribbled a plan on an index card, and ran to the dollar store a couple of hours before the meeting with the only two dollars I had in my pocket to pick up supplies. Somehow, I managed to pull it off. We did collage, made chef's hats and then put on a skit. That night, as Patrick was tucking him in, our Cub Scout said, "You know what I want to be when I grow up, Daddy?"

I paused to eavesdrop in the hall, expecting a new elaboration on his recent ambition to become a night watchman at the museum.

"What?"

"A Cub Scout den leader." Peeking around the corner, I could see his eyes were shining. I thought my heart would just give out then and there. Never before have I been his hero.

The memory of that moment is the winch that hauled me out of the ditch today. That, and watching my son's eyes shine again as his father—frequently the hero—sawed and carved his pencil sketch into three-dimensional race car reality, complete with tailfins and a chrome paint job. Somehow, he managed to pull it off.

Somehow, I guess we always do.

Kyran Pittman pulls it off daily at www.notestoself.us

If They Only Knew

"Sometimes I lock myself in the bathroom."

As a new mother, I succumbed to my young daughter Phoebe's every fashion whim. As a toddler, she was obsessed with a standard pink leotard with a prickly tulle tutu and she insisted on wearing it everywhere. I mean everywhere. But I was so enamored of her independent style that I even helped her accessorize it with a cotton turtleneck so she could move seamlessly from fall to winter when the temperature dropped. Eventually, her beloved ensemble morphed into a series of Spice Girls–inspired outfits— flared leggings and rhinestone-festooned shirts, several riding high above her midriff.

It seemed adorable until it wasn't. And it wasn't when one day I looked up at her and thought, "Oh, my God, my little girl looks like a stripper."

My emotions were a jumble. I had created this "monster." I'd given in to the whining at the store and purchased clingy, glittery items despite my better judgment and fashion sense. I admit it, she wasn't the only one attracted to these "must-have" pieces; at the time I actually thought a pint-sized version of a sexy starlet was cute. But now I'd come to my senses. My daughter's belly was soft and round and to me, irresistible, but it certainly didn't need to be paraded around the playground, swaddled in sparkles and spandex.

Desperate times required desperate measures. Given that there was no way my daughter was going to give up her glitzy uniforms without a fight (and also given the fact that I wasn't up to fighting), I brought in an element that would take things out of our hands: red nail polish. I splattered an entire bottle across her favorite items leaving an army of angry red blotches everywhere. When she discovered the stained clothing in her closet, I shared her shock and disbelief and then we had a somber, brief ceremony when they were disposed of in the trash. It wasn't until recently, as we packed up her room to send her off to college that I came clean about my dirty trick. Thankfully, we both had a good laugh.

As mothers, we become crafty and resourceful, and resort to thoughts and actions we never thought possible. Who knew I could stoop so low as to actively deface my kid's clothing? Not me. But at the time, it seemed like the only option and a clever one at that. As seen in the confessional, we moms are brilliant at conjuring shortcuts (cleaning up that spill with our pants legs) and coping mechanisms (a little vodka in the thermos at a never-ending baseball game) to get through our days and to tackle situations in our harried lives for which there are no how-to lists. Sometimes our "creativity" is worthy of sharing. Yet often, it might be worth sharing, but certainly not with anyone we live with or could bump into at the next birthday party.

The confessional offers an alternative—a chance to unload the embarrassing and the shameful, the creative and the crass. In this chapter it's clear that there are some things we can't, won't or shouldn't tell our kids, our partners or our friends. But it's my belief that everything can be shared anonymously in cyberspace, because you never know when one mom's secret might be another mom's solace or even a solution—something that can help her get through a long day or even longer night and even if only briefly, let her know that she's not alone.

I bite my baby daughter's fingernails off rather than using clippers.

We held a PTA meeting at my house last week. All the moms marveled at my clean home. Thank God they didn't look too closely: I'd put all the dirty dishes in the oven and stuffed the overflowing piles of dirty clothes (and the stinky dog bed) in the hall closet!

Often, when I'm trying to figure out what to do with regard to my little girl, I think of my parents and what they would do. And then I do the exact opposite.

Sometimes when I spill something on my kitchen floor, I just "mop" it up with the bottom of my pants leg as I walk by.

41

I "lost" DD's favorite book because I was tired of doing the different voices a hundred times a day.

The other night, I was informed at 10 PM that my daughter Olivia needed a Chinese food dish for a class project first thing the next morning. So I turned the dogs' home-cooked chicken and rice meal—same stuff we eat, but still, prepped for the dogs—into "Gourmet Fried Rice," with fried tofu, water chestnuts and broccoli. I congratulated myself on my creativity, but still felt guilty, I suppose because I hadn't made pork dumplings by hand, with pig I'd slaughtered myself . . . Ah, parenting . . .

When people notice the improvement in my son's behavior, I tell them it's because I cut red dye and refined sugar out of his diet. Actually, it's because I started seeing a therapist and stopped yelling at him so much, but how do I explain that?

Have you ever seen the show *Weeds*? That's me. We live in suburbia, have a very happy, albeit semi-dysfunctional little family, I am a fourth-year university student, my husband owns a successful business . . . but we happen to sell marijuana out of the little house that my grandmother left us several years ago. We make a lot of money and it's hard to stop. We'd be pretty well off without that income, but with it we have it *made*.

I went back to work so that I would yell at my coworkers instead of my son.

Sometimes when I'm at the supermarket with my son in his stroller, I "forget" to pay for a thing or two I stuck in the stroller basket.

My husband works in a high-risk job. Sometimes I find myself daydreaming about what it would be like if he died at work, and what I would do with the life insurance money. God, I'm a horrible person.

I joined Weight Watchers just so that I would have a place to go by myself once a week.

49

My mom raised me to be a strong, independent, do-it-yourself woman. We installed air conditioners together, mowed the lawn, worked the BBQ and replaced all the electrical outlets in the kitchen. She moved me in and out of both of my last two apartments without my dad's help, and regularly takes vacations by herself. It would kill her to know that I have no interest in working sixty hours a week as a lawyer and just want to get married to a wealthy man so I don't have to worry about money.

I haven't taught my kids to tell time yet . . . that way I can say it's bedtime whenever I want.

People at the daycare where my daughter goes kept telling me what a lovely shade of strawberry blonde her hair is today. It's extra orange from the pasta sauce she smeared in it last night that I just tried to brush over rather than wash out.

Sometimes I am just so sick of doing laundry that I keep drying loads of clothes over and over again just so I don't have to put them away. I'll let the hubby do it!

When I forget my ChapStick, I use my Lansinoh nipple cream instead.

I got pregnant so I could get a break from working every day.

I smother my six-year-old with kisses and hugs every day because I am so scared that when he is a teenager he will hate me.

I pretend I'm still asleep in the morning when my husband is getting ready for work so I don't have to talk to him.

IF THEY ONLY KNEW

Once when my son was teething, we had nothing to numb his gums so we used "Pleasure Balm" from our Kama Sutra set. Funny thing was ... it worked better than Oragel.

When I'm mad at my husband I take all of his socks and roll them into one big, huge sock ball. It's amusing to me to have him go through all of them to find the match. Oh, it's the little things!

59

When I am getting really frustrated with the kids, I try to sit down and look through photo albums. Just seeing their gorgeous, smiling faces and all the silly things they've done makes my heart melt. It restores my faith that this, too, will pass and they will return to being my angels once more.

Sometimes late at night when everyone is sleeping, I put on my headphones and turn up my iPod. Then I dance around the room imagining for a little while that I am some famous pop tartlet lip-synching a song. It sounds stupid, but I look forward to my "imagination" time. It almost makes me feel like I have a secret life and even though I know it is only make-believe, it makes me feel good inside to just pretend I am someone other than a mom for a little while.

I am a SAHM and I love it . . . my secret shame though? When I'm goofing off on the Internet, I pretend I'm at a huge office doing very important paperwork and filing . . . makes me feel less guilty about spending so much time on the Internet.

I lean over my babies' beds at night when they're asleep and whisper, "I promise I'll be a better mommy tomorrow." There are just too many days I wish I'd done better.

Sometimes I pretend cameras are following me around in my everyday life. It makes the most mundane tasks more exciting. Like, I can pretend I'm on a cooking show when making dinner. Or shooting a music video when I sing in the car picking the kids up from school. I even imagine Dr. Phil's cameras are there when my kids are misbehaving so that I'm calmer when dealing with them.

Sometimes when I'm holding my beautiful baby in my arms and we're gazing lovingly at each other, I secretly wish that she would fall asleep so that I could check my e-mail.

I eat all the marshmallows out of the Lucky Charms.

I play Guitar Hero after my kids leave for school because I want to finally beat them with a higher score!

IF THEY ONLY KNEW

I wish someone had told me . . .

I wish someone had told me that they sleep through the night eventually. Those first few weeks home from the hospital with my first baby were not an experience I'd care to relive. Ever.

I wish someone had told me what an ass my ex-DH really was. I wish I had never married him.

I wish someone had told me how hard it would be to be a stepmother. Especially when the biological mother sucks. I wish that I was his son's mom and we never had to deal with his ex-wife.

I wish someone had told me that life is never like the movies. Time is more precious than diamonds. You should always treat the ones you love better than you treat strangers. And never lose the fun person you are, because she is what makes this all worth it.

I wish someone had told me that it is "different when they're your own." You bet they are—you can't give them back to their parents when you've had enough!

"Lovelorn"

by Bumble Ward

I try not to think too much about N going away to college on Friday. I'm taking him to New York on the trusty
JetBlue and I will return on Sunday without him. When
it does come up, a small lump appears in my throat and
I have to suck my cheeks in order to prevent the tears
from welling up. It feels as if all of this has happened far
too soon, that only a couple of months ago he was a little boy with a pudding-bowl haircut (I don't know what I
was thinking) and a best friend called Joseph, who liked
Power Rangers and Ninja Turtles and was scared of the
garbage truck.

He's so tall now that I reach his chest, and yesterday
when we all played in the pool, I climbed on him for a pig-
gyback ride and he felt like a huge giant, with big mus-

cles. There is so much goodness in the core of him, that it makes me feel like a bad person in comparison. There is truth zooming out of every pore, like great wonky shafts of light, along with his absolute sense of right and wrong and what is fair in the world, and who is being treated with injustice. I can't fight with him anymore, because usually his argument is better thought out than mine (the rhetoric major doesn't fall far from the tree). And when we do argue, as we did this morning, because I was complaining that he was being negative, all I wanted to do was sweep him up in my arms and tell him that I love him.

Oh how sweet the regret. How I wish that it had been me who took him to the swimming hole when he was a small child, and not the nanny; instead I was in my office stuck on a no-doubt-useless conference call. How I wish it had been me who picked him up from school every day and heard about his day. God bless those mothers who truly believe they can have it all, because I don't believe it; I think we kid ourselves into thinking that way, brainwash ourselves, in fact.

The English part of me just wants to suck it up and carry on. And another part is laughing at my weepy self, all self-pity and icky-ness and this constant desire to throw my arms around him. But I can't help but think that this is the end of something wonderful, as well as the beginning of something new and probably equally amazing, but it's the end part I'm dwelling on now. I want to say prayers and wrap up care packages in brown paper and stare at him like a lovelorn terrier. I want to tell him that I'm so proud of him that it's bursting my buttons. And I want to tell him that this, too, will pass, and that even though it seems scary now, soon that smile will be back on his face and we'll all be laughing together again.

Bumble Ward documents it all at www.misswhistle.com

My Body, Myself

"I am NOT squishy."

Wrestling on the bed one day, my daughter pinned me down and, giggling, sat atop my bottom while tickling my belly. "Mom, you are just so squishy!" she said. My tush became her bongo drum and she patted and chanted, "Squishy, squishy, squishy!"

Thank God my face was buried in the pillow. I felt like ejecting her off my back, and telling her that "squishy" was a word for Play-Doh, not for Mommy. But with the responsibility of helping her and her sister develop a healthy relationship with their bodies ("squishy" or otherwise), I simply laughed it off.

We mothers are shape-shifters. Our bodies stretch and transform and through the bearing and caring of children, they morph from form to function. On a good day, I can appreciate the miracles and mysteries of my flesh. If I try hard enough, I can embrace my fuller hips and softer stomach. If I squint, my stretch marks can look beautiful. If I keep the lights dim in the closet, cup my breasts and hoist them up to where they used to be, I like what I see. But aging and twenty-seven months of gestation has taken its toll and there's often a disconnect between how I feel—twenty-eight and able to wear a bikini—and how I look: forty-five and OK in a one piece (as long as it has good support).

It's clear from this chapter that I'm not alone in wondering, "Who is that woman staring back at me in the mirror?" Some moms lament not recognizing themselves postpartum, one exclaiming, "A fat woman ate me!"; another wondering how her mother's body could have replaced her own, seemingly overnight. On the other end of the spectrum are the moms surprised yet celebrating their new curves and discovering that only after giving birth did they finally feel at home in their bodies.

For me, I often wax nostalgic for the days when I didn't have to worry about jeans being cut so low that they ride dangerously close to my C-section scar, or when I could throw on a white T-shirt without needing a spandex tank top underneath to keep everything tucked in just so. But really, these days are better ones; my body did the hard and amazing work of bringing three wonderful, healthy kids into my life and for that, a little wear and tear is a very small price to pay.

I have a great face. I have beautiful hair. I dress nice. I smell nice. I am funny and smart and witty and biting and caring and polite and ballsy and poetic and strong. My husband loves me, my kids love me, my coworkers love me, my friends love me. So why is it that the only thing I see in the mirror is my belly? Why do those extra 40 pounds take away from everything else? Why do I let them?

MY BODY, MYSELF

I weigh 215 pounds, but today for some reason I felt so damn sexy!

Before I moved into a new area I had a tummy tuck and breast implants. All my new friends think I look this good because I work out! I've never told them my secret because I know they'd talk behind my back!

Eating comforts me when he doesn't.

Why is it my husband can call me fat, lazy and stupid and I believe him? And more important, why am I so afraid to leave him?

Oh, what I wouldn't give for liposuction and a tummy tuck.

I secretly think I am beautiful. I have not lost the 25 pounds of pregnancy weight, but I put my clothes on over my curves, look in the mirror before leaving in the morning, and think I am stunningly gorgeous, tossing away any idea of losing weight. Then I get to the park and see all the skinny yuppie and hipster mothers and instantly feel fat. I wish I could hold on to that morning moment all the time.

I nursed and now my boobs are in a race to see which one will hit my belly button first...the left one is winning.

I'm overweight. My stomach is covered with stretch marks and is saggy and squishy from recent weight loss. My boobs are saggy. My hips are disproportionately large. My thighs jiggle. My underarms wave way after I stop. And despite all this, I love my body and can't understand why everyone always wants me to change it!

I was folding laundry yesterday and came across a pair of panties that were mine. My loving son (age eight) said, "There is no way those are yours, Mom. You are too fat to fit into them." I haven't eaten since.

I just lied to the woman at Victoria's Secret about why I need to be measured for a new bra. I told her I just had a baby. That was twenty months ago. Then she had to break the news that they don't sell my new size there, and I would be better off at Lane Bryant.

MY BODY, MYSELF

I was thirty-four years old when I had my second and last baby over four years ago. That pregnancy ruined my body. Now I am very fat and officially have a belly apron. A big one.

I thought that if I lost weight I'd feel better about myself. I had gastric bypass, lost almost 120 pounds and guess what? I still hate my body. Now I look like a huge white elephant that had the air sucked out of it. When will it ever be enough?

I blame this extra weight on my son but I had it before.

I am fat and glorious. I won't let anyone tell me otherwise on either account. I make it all happen around here and I do it with style. My big ass is good at everything I need to do. That's all I'm saying.

MY BODY, MYSELF

I am back in my fat jeans!!! Waaaah!!!

The other day my DH decided to point out that I was really getting a lot of grays. Boy, that made me feel great. I'm only twenty-eight! Why doesn't he ever notice something positive?

MY BODY, MYSELF

DD's age: 9 months.

Pounds gained during pregnancy: 37

Times I've exercised since: 0

Current pants size: 0

Benefits of nursing: priceless

I've lost 117 pounds; why do I still feel fat?

Sometimes I check out my teenage daughter's body and get jealous. Most of the time though I am amazed I made someone that is so beautiful.

I love my body. I love the breasts that fed my daughters. I love the stretch marks that show where my babies grew. I love the belly and thighs that are bigger, like an African fertility goddess. I even like that I have gained weight with the medications that I am on because those medications have saved my life. I love my hair that is long—almost to my waist and I love my freckles. I love my dimple. I love ME!

I overheard a little girl tease my daughter for having a fat mom. DD (age five) replied, "My mom's fat but she's still way prettier than your mom!!" I have the best kid ever.

I never thought I'd say . . .

**"Tell me that's toothpaste on the
wall and not your boogie."**

"Why on earth did you pierce
your own lip?"

"When you're done peeing, give it
a little shake. But don't shake it
too much cuz then you're
just playing with it."

"Don't sit on your sister's head."

"Put your underwear on. I'm tired
of seeing your ding-a-ling!"

97

True Mom Poll

Post-baby, what part of your body is making you crazy?

Saggy breasts: 10%

Wiggly tummy: **49%**

Hippier hips: 2%

None of the above—I love my new bod! 7%

All of the above—where, oh where,
did my body go? 31%

"My hips, my thighs, my breasts, my belly"

by Catherine Connors

Before I had my first baby, I didn't give my body much thought. I had always been naturally slim and well-proportioned, and had always taken that for granted. I had never bemoaned the size of my breasts or hips or tummy; I never went on a diet or worried about going to the gym. I just didn't give it any thought. I didn't have to. My body was just there, and it was fine, so, whatever.

Such is the luxury of youth. Such is the luxury of a body that has not witnessed the rigors of breeding, child-bearing, breastfeeding and the tearing of one's nether regions.

When I had my first baby, I gained over sixty pounds. I didn't worry about it. It would go away. My body had never had extra weight on it, and I didn't expect it to tolerate the intrusion now. So I just waited for it to go away. It didn't. So I tried to learn to love it, or at least ignore it. I couldn't.

The funny thing was, though, that in trying to come to terms with a body that was no longer low-maintenance, I got to know that body better. I had never had an intimate relationship with my perfect, youthful body. I hadn't needed to. So I didn't really know it. But this body, this stretch-marked, lumpy, heavy-breasted, imperfect body—*this* body I got to know. Intimately. I became acquainted with my torn and scarred vulva, my lactation-weary and chewed-upon breasts. With my stretch-marked hips, and with my decidedly nonflat stomach. With the extra padding around my upper arms, and with the place where my thighs now rub together.

And with that intimacy—that ambivalent intimacy— came a sort of erotic charge that I'd never known before. My hips, my thighs, my breasts, my belly: all were now imperfect, and alien. But that alienness forced me to introduce myself to them, to get to know them, to meet them, touch them and understand them, and that, I learned, was hot. Somehow, unexpectedly, my big, battered maternal body became beautiful—erotically beautiful—to me in a way that my perfect youthful beauty never could, because of its perfection.

I'm pregnant again, and have moments of fear about

100

the future of this body, my body. Will I still find some erotic beauty in breasts that are even further battered, in a belly that is even bigger? Will I end up at the gym, trying to force my body back to its banal perfection? Or will I just turn the lights out, run my hands over the ample flesh of my breasts and down the dimpled landscape of my thighs to the places that are all the more sensitive for having been torn by nature, and embrace these as erotically, messily mine?

I don't know. But I'd like to think that it will be the latter.

Catherine flaunts her flaws at www.herbadmother.com

Do As I Say,
Not As I Do

"And then I threw it at him."

I'm still undecided about the nature versus nurture debate—unclear as to how much of my children's fate is already locked and loaded in the twisted strands of their DNA and how much sway I have on their nimble, impressionable minds. But whether I rank above or beneath their peers as a key influencer, I would argue that I'm high on the list. Monkey see, monkey do and I should know better than to behave badly in front of them or, worse, create rules and blatantly break them. And I confess: I break my own rules on a regular basis. Just last week I was three-for-three in the "do as I say, not as I do" game that I unwittingly play with my children.

My first offense was brought to my attention when my teenage daughter Phoebe attacked me for my housekeeping hypocrisy. She told me I had no right berating her for the minefield of a mess in her room when my closet (which she happened to waltz into unannounced) was equally offensive. She was leaving for college in a week so she had an excuse (this time at least), but did I? No. She darted around the closet picking up and dropping pants left on the floor as I often did in her room complete with a face pinched with disappointment and disgust. She pointed out opened drawers, even an open Diet Coke can on the top of the dresser. Touché.

My son Owen followed suit and ratted me out to his sister Annabel about my calling a truly deserving driver a "F%*king a$%hole" while taking him to a playdate. She then decided to top him with my latest faux pas: eating with my fingers while standing in front of an open refrigerator.

Despite our best intentions, we mothers are often doing one thing and saying another. We know the stakes are high; that we are the primary role models for our young charges. Yet in big and small ways, we bend or break the rules and don't play fair. And who could blame us? Sometimes, in moments of desperation, rage or simply forgetting who the adult is and reverting to rebellious children ourselves, we lose our tempers, leave the lights on or lick the bowl.

I'm sometimes surprised (but always grateful) that my kids will forgive and often forget my transgressions. They still look to me to guide the way, set the course and keep them safe. And I've recently realized that often, when I'm caught in the harsh light of hypocrisy, it gives my kids the opportunity to step in and set me straight. They become the teachers, so even while I'm doing something wrong, I'm comforted by knowing that I've done something right.

Last night my son threw his pacifier. I was tired and frustrated and said, "We don't throw things!" And then I threw it at him.

The other day my four-year-old would not stop crying at every little thing. I was so frustrated I grabbed him by his shoulders and yelled loudly at him to stop. "Just stop. Use your words and stop acting like a baby." Then I sent him to his room. I feel like an ass because I had a tantrum and lost control. When I went in his room to apologize he told me he was sorry and that he wanted to start his day over. It broke my heart and I hate myself for it.

I get mad when my kids bother me while I am trying to read a book—about being a better parent.

I forgot to pick my kids up at school!

DO AS I SAY, NOT AS I DO

I posed nude for a pinup website and I'm really worried about what I'll tell my girls in the future when I'm preaching about respecting themselves.

I treasure my three hours in the afternoon to myself so much that I would rather drag all four kids with me to the grocery store, than give up my afternoon "me time" to do it. While they are in school, I sit around playing Xbox .

DO AS I SAY, NOT AS I DO

I think I'm an alcoholic. I don't get sloppy drunk, pass out, drive drunk, or engage in risky behavior, but I must have two to four drinks every night or else I feel anxious and panicky. I don't know how to stop it. I hate that I'm setting such a bad example for my kids, but if I don't have my wine at the end of the day, I feel like I'm going to have a panic attack.

I cry in my car. A lot.

DO AS I SAY, NOT AS I DO

I bribe my kids with candy to get them to behave at the grocery store.

My daughter has apparently inherited my oral fixation. This is a bad thing, as I am twenty-four years old and still battling it. I feel like the biggest hypocrite when I scold her for using her brother's pacifier or sucking on or chewing paper and crayons, when at night I suck my thumb before falling asleep.

Today a man at the car wash told me I was a bad example for my kids because I let them stand on a bench in their muddy shoes. When he said, "Why don't you clean up after yourself?" I said, "Why don't you stop being such an asshole?" Then my three-year-old daughter yelled, "Yeah! Why don't you stop being such a jerk?"

I can tell my kids no, but I can't tell myself no. I am such a hypocrite. At least I know why they are thin and I'm 330 pounds.

I wish someone had told me . . .

I wish someone had told me that having kids is the end of my life. Everything now is about them; there is no more "me" and if I try to have any "me" time, I'm called selfish.

I wish someone had told me that everyone is screwed up in one way or another, no matter how pulled together they look from the outside. And that those who don't have any screws loose are very boring.

I wish someone had told me that a size 8 is not huge. I'm in a 14 now and would give anything to get back down to an 8!

I wish someone had told me that "getting revenge" for my husband's affair would slowly eat at my self-respect as well as completely ruin any and all of my sex drive. I got herpes as an added bonus!

I wish someone had told me how quickly the time flies and your kids become adults.

"I am still vain and would like to be irreplaceable."

by Leah Peterson

When people get married, they don't expect to get divorced. We were no different. My first husband and I were determined to make it work and we fought it out for almost fourteen years. We would tell each other, "We can do this! We'll figure it out because we are strong enough to make it work!" When we finally reached the breaking point, there was nothing I wanted more than for him to marry someone else who would love him and my kids. We ended as some odd sort of friends with a long and varied past, and had the best in mind for each other.

I wanted his new wife—because there was no question that he would be getting married right away—to really, really, really love the kids and be there for them. I wanted my kids to feel like she was their *other* real mom. To trust her. To love her. And maybe that was odd because in a way, it could be looked at as if she were replacing me. But for them to be in a real family would be the best thing for them. For them to have anything less might be detrimental and there was never a moment when I wished for that.

Over the past few years, their stepmom has been everything I wished and hoped for. We might not be best friends, and that is most likely a much more healthy relationship than I had originally imagined, but we are always more than civil and most of the time slightly warm. And the kids think of her as their mom. They call us both "Mom" interchangeably and within the same breath. To them, they are safe in their relationship with both of us and have no reason to differentiate with a *step* here or a *bio* there unless there is someone else in the conversation who really doesn't get it. Then you might hear one of them backing up a bit to explain who is who. Maybe. But it's just as likely they won't take the time to explain and figure it is that person's problem if he or she doesn't get it.

And oddly, there is nothing that I'm prouder of. And still, there is nothing that pierces my heart quite like hearing them call her "Mom." It's a strange, revealing moment to be feeling discomfort and then in a shocked second remember that it's something you wished for. Because on some level, I am still vain and would like to be irreplaceable. I'd like to be the only "Mom" in their life and have them depend on me for all of their mom needs. And she could be there, doing a really fine job of being a *step* mom, but I would be the *real* "Mom." This is the fantasy that rides through my brain from time to time. But sadly, it isn't reality. And *thankfully*, it isn't reality. Because being safe on all sides is what is best for them. And I'm happy they call her "Mom" even when my heart occasionally bleeds a bit on the inside where they can't see. Maybe hers does, too.

Leah Peterson is safe on all sides at www.leahpeah.com

Judge, Jury and Executioner

"That's not breast milk, it's nondairy creamer."

My best friend nursed her kids until they were close to two years old. So it was only natural that with her as my main mommy role model at the time—along with the selection of preachy newborn books I'd ingested during a long stint on bed rest—that I, too, would breastfeed my daughter as long as I possibly could.

Ah, the best-laid plans . . .

Nursing did not come easily to me—not at all the way they said it would in the books. From day one, my daughter had trouble latching on, my nipples were sore and cracked, and I spent more time on the phone with the kind, but slightly patronizing La Leche League women who attempted to talk me through the ways of guiding my engorged boob into my daughter's tiny mouth. They gave me pep talks and encouraged me to keep going with their sing-songy mantra, "Breast is best!"

I admit that I had a few weeks of that slightly drugged, warm feeling you get when your milk lets down and mother and child do indeed feel like one. These moments, however, were fleeting and after six weeks I threw in the towel. But I didn't tell anyone. Not my husband and not my friends.

I introduced a bottle into my daughter's life, explaining that I couldn't be the only milk in town (I had a job to get back to!), but continued to excuse myself to "pump" up in the privacy of my bedroom where I would flip the switch on the two-pronged electric sucking machine and promptly take a nap. To cover my tracks further, I filled the small plastic breast milk bags with a little nondairy creamer and water and kept several in the refrigerator and freezer just in case my friends dropped by. One day, one of them even commented on how lucky I was to be producing so much milk.

Why did I keep up such a ruse? Because at the time, I was exhausted and overwhelmed and I couldn't bear the thought of being judged or scrutinized for my choice. I was already beating myself up for "failing"; I certainly didn't need to take the heat from anyone else.

From spanking, contributing to overpopulation, serving sodas and cookies, or choosing to work while raising your kids—the sharp current of judgment runs strong and steady among mothers. We know better; that we're only fueling the mommy wars and making the hard jobs we do even harder. But while moms don't fess up on the playground or the office or the PTA meeting, we're all guilty of thinking less than kind thoughts and belittling different choices as a way to justify our own.

It's fine to disagree on parenting philosophies, but my hope is that by encouraging moms to go online and purge themselves of judgmental thoughts, maybe—just maybe—we can encourage a little more acceptance when we're face-to-face.

After all the drama I've seen in my twenty-plus years in the workforce and now on my mommy message boards, I've come to the realization that no matter how old we get, we never really leave high school.

TRUE MOM CONFESSIONS

Why is it that other people think they can comment on another person's reproductive life? The whole "Oh, not going to try for a girl?" thing or "Going to try for a boy?" thing gets on my nerves. I have a boy and a girl, so what? My family is perfect? I'd love them no matter what, and if they'd both been girls, we would have been done anyway. Unless someone else wants to step up and help raise those kids, shut up. How many kids I have, or don't have, is between me and Hubby.

JUDGE, JURY AND EXECUTIONER

Are *The Simpsons* really that bad for a two-year-old? I mean she's not really watching it and all I did was forget to change the channel when it came on. Why do you have to give me shit about my parenting all the time? Thanks, Mom.

I join all the political groups on Facebook so my online friends don't think I'm stupid because I'm "just" a SAHM.

I think people who don't "believe" in ADHD, autism, or other psychological disorders are ignorant and judgmental. Just because you're lucky enough not to have to deal with one of these challenges yourself doesn't mean the disorders don't exist. And discounting the knowledge and testimonials of huge numbers of doctors, psychologists, and affected people is really arrogant. The icing on the cake? Those who pat themselves on the back about their superior parenting skills because their child "doesn't behave like that." Trust me, I am a GREAT mother. You would end up in tears in a heap on the floor if you had to parent my kid every day.

I'm breast-feeding my sixteen-month-old and I don't care if you think it's gross. It's wonderful. She loves it, I love it, and it keeps me thin.

JUDGE, JURY AND EXECUTIONER

I wish someone could create a magic potion to make kids behave in public. If we spank, we're looked at like we're Satan. If we DON'T spank, people think we're too "soft" on our kids. Moms are judged unfairly no matter what we do.

I hate when I read anything about formula-feeding mommies being judged for their decision to use formula. So what?! If the kid's happy and healthy, then what does it matter?!

JUDGE, JURY AND EXECUTIONER

The only reason I work is to pay the bills. I would stay home with her in a heartbeat. But I tell people that I work so that I still connect with adults, so they don't judge me.

I hate it when women who have no children judge my parenting.

Before you judge me for NOT breast-feeding my son, why not take a moment and listen to WHY I didn't do it. After all, we are all mothers who do what is best for our children. Every child is different, and as a mother, we know what is best for our baby. So, before you call me "selfish" or a "bad mom," why not listen to me? I feed my baby and that is all that matters. It doesn't matter if it's breast milk or formula. What matters is, I love my son more than my own life, and would do anything for him. So please, don't judge me and call me horrid names just because I didn't breast-feed.

Those of you who feel judged for not wanting another child are not alone. I am being judged because I am still trying (after two failures) to adopt another child. People keep telling me to "just be happy with the one you have."

I'm having a breast augmentation after Easter and I haven't told anyone in my family yet. I know they'd be quick to judge. I've only shared it with one coworker since I will be out for a few days. I really don't want the gossip to be about me—can I just have some big boobs in peace???

I'm a grown woman, so why do I still care what my dad thinks of me? He's visiting in a few days and I'm running around making sure everything is perfect for him because I know he will judge me when he gets here. Ugh!

JUDGE, JURY AND EXECUTIONER

My seven-year-old has an IQ of 92 and the normal for her age is 50. I am very proud 'cause she isn't a dork, she is very pretty, and all the kids in her class love her. So why is it that everyone I tell is quick to judge her?

My daughter gets sort of touchy-feely with her girl-friends when they come over for playdates. It makes me uncomfortable and I tell her to back off and she does. I talked to a friend of mine (who is a lesbian) about when she knew she was gay. She asked me why I wanted to know and I told her about the playdate behavior. Now I feel like I've betrayed my kid some-how. I honestly don't think my daughter is gay (not that I would ever love her any less even if she were), but I was looking for perspective. Now I feel bad about the whole thing, like my friend will say something to someone else and judge her based on something I, her MOM, said. (My daughter is ten by the way.)

I hate that people assume I used fertility drugs just because I had multiples. I don't judge others who used them but hate the idea that people think *I* did.

How dare you yell at me in the middle of Wal-Mart that I am going to burn in hell because I have tattoos and piercings! So what if my hair is multicolored? When I offered to go get my Bible out of my truck to discuss it with you like adults you finally left me the hell alone. You don't know me and neither does anyone else in this hypocritical, holier-than-thou, inbred little town! You have no clue that my daughter is the top student in her school, that I care for a critically ill parent, and that I have been a loving and devoted wife for thirteen years while raising my daughter and two nieces! I thought Christianity had some small thing in it about not judging others lest ye be judged. Ring a freakin' bell??

JUDGE, JURY AND EXECUTIONER

I have been called an idiot and judgmental more than one time on my mommy board. These people don't like me because...I am...(*gasp*)...a Republican. Then these moms go on to blame me for everything from the Iraq war to the bad economy. I had nothing to do with those things; heck, I didn't even vote for G.W.! Either time.

Maybe it's wrong, but I judge other moms by how clean their kids are . . . dirty kid = bad mom. Is it seriously that hard to break out a wipe and take the crud off your kid's face?

JUDGE, JURY AND EXECUTIONER

So . . . you think that a person who needs to use food stamps shouldn't be able to get ice cream and chips for their kid's birthday party? I wish people would lose the judgment when they see someone in line using food stamps.

People wrongly assume that I am against abortion because I decided to continue a very obviously unplanned pregnancy. It drives me CRAZY. They even go so far as to talk crap to me about women they/we know who have had abortions. Ugh, I don't really want to be a part of your hateful, judgmental club, thank you!

I never thought I'd say . . .

**"Actually, I like your hair the blue-green
color best, but this pinky-purple
doesn't look that bad either."**

"Bend over so I can spray your butt.
No, all the way over, touch your toes.
Now, open your butt."

"That's not a Tootsie Roll, it's
cat poop, spit it out."

**"If you don't get up off the floor
I am gonna leave you here
and get a new baby!!"**

True Mom Poll

Have you ever asked your kids
to keep a secret from your spouse?

Yes, I have and I don't think there's
anything wrong with it! 10%

Yes, but not very often: 24%

Nope. My kids can't keep secrets from anybody: 14%

Nope. Sets a bad example: **44%**

None of the above: 8%

"More like Fast Food Fanny"

by Beth Feldman

If there were an Olympic category for multitasking, I would be the gold medal champion hands-down. When I start my day each morning, I consider my forty-five-minute regimen a race against the clock to get everything done without the kids being late for school or missing my commuter train.

Sometimes, I purposely give myself less time in the morning just to see if I can break my personal best record. I know I'm warped, but if you're curious to find out exactly what I can accomplish each morning, well, here's a snapshot:

6:45 AM   Wake up. Turn over. Go back to sleep.
7:00 AM   Wake up again for real.

7:10 AM   Shower. Remind myself to get razors. Haven't shaved for weeks. Think of fifty-five things I need to accomplish today and come up with an idea for a killer business.

7:20 AM   Apply makeup, get dressed, blow dry and flatiron hair.

7:30 AM   Tell kids to get up, continue blow drying.

7:35 AM   Call out to kids again to wake up. Continue styling hair. Collar seems a bit wrinkly. Use flatiron to straighten collar.

7:40 AM   Scream at kids to wake up. No luck.

7:45 AM   Bribe kids with money to get up. It works.

7:50 AM   Daughter refuses to wear pants I've selected because they're too short. Select three more outfits, agree on an ensemble that's acceptable to her.

7:52 AM   Pick out clothes for my son. Pants must go on first, then T-shirt, then socks—in that order. If I dare put his shirt on first, we must take off clothes and get him dressed in the proper order or risk having naked child in kindergarten class.

7:55 AM   Breakfast buffet for kids: Lucky Charms, frozen waffles, Pop-Tarts. I never said I was Betty Crocker. More like Fast Food Fanny.

7:56 AM Realize that it's "no junk food" week at school. Take a bite out of a chocolate waffle, grab carton of eggs and whip up a batch of huevos rancheros for *los ninos.* Who am I kidding? Make two scrambled eggs and call it a day.

8:00 AM Forgot to order groceries online so I hand my daughter three bucks for hot lunch and pray my son will eat last night's chow fun special from Hunan Ritz. (They have microwaves in school—I'm not that heartless.)

8:07 AM Fill out forms for upcoming class trip. Find checkbook, pay for class trip. Volunteer to be class parent on said class trip because daughter is begging me to attend. Realize I've got another appointment that day but will figure out how to make it work when I get closer to that date.

8:10 AM Check homework and see glaring errors in daughter's reading assignment. Whip out eraser from kitchen utensil drawer and attempt to write like a third grader. See she forgot to answer two questions—attempt to think like a third-grader.

8:11 AM Alert. There's a juice spill in the den. Need paper towels stat! Can feel steam blowing out of ears. Bring in paper towels, Clorox wipes, and a Swiffer (all in one hand) and tell kids not to spill juice in the den again—they give forty-nine excuses why it wasn't their fault and I tell them that tomorrow, they eat in the kitchen . . . now that's a concept!

8:15 AM   Remind kids to brush teeth, brush hair, put on jackets, scarves and mittens.

8:20 AM   Hit the garage. Strap everyone in seats and we are out the door.

And that's a typical morning. Sometimes I'm even dealing with a writing deadline of my own in the middle of the mayhem, and while I may seem like I am on autopilot, I'm actually in serious training mode. You never know when the Olympic Committee will decide to open up a category for multitasking moms. And if that ever happens, I want to be ready.

See Beth Feldman multitask at www.rolemommy.com

There Is No "I" in Mommy

"Mommies don't cry."

I stood in the middle of the alphabet rug with my first-born, Phoebe, who was three years old. She was wailing, her nose running, her face hot and sticky with tears. She buried her head in the pleats of my skirt and held my legs in a viselike grip. It was the first day of "preschool separation" and while all the other parents had made a quick getaway, there I was, the last mom standing.

A few tentative toddlers looked at us, tears threatening to fall each time Phoebe let out one of her sobs. This was not good. Finally, a teacher came up to us and gently peeled Phoebe off my body, motioning me toward the door. "Do. Not. Look Back." She whispered to me through a smile, "It will make it much worse for both of you."

I did as I was told and, in a daze, stumbled down the hall to the coffee room where a group of other parents sat checking their date books (no cell phones yet in 1993) and fidgeting nervously. The school director walked in, greeted us with a kind yet slightly patronizing look and high-lighted the milestone moment we were experiencing. Our precious toddlers would be fine. Just fine. Good-bye tears were perfectly normal.

My hand shot up from the crowd and despite the lump in my throat I uttered, "But what if I need to cry?"

Her warm expression turned cold and she said firmly, "You take it outside. Mommies don't cry here."

I nodded my head, acknowledging that I understood that right here, right now, I was the grown-up and I needed to keep my emotions in check. I then politely excused myself and ran sobbing into the bathroom where I sat, head in hands, on a child-sized toilet feeling sad, scared and alone.

Through my early years as a mother, I found this lack of an outlet for my often confusing, embarrassing or unex-pected emotions to be the rule and not the exception. So I, like many other mothers, took the path of least resistance and pushed them aside. I became a caretaker of others, but blatantly neglected to care for myself. I diligently went to pediatrician appointments but couldn't get to the gym. I thought about the newest Nickelodeon programming and stopped watching the national news. I worried that my kids wouldn't make friends while my own friendships shifted and many slipped away.

From the confessions in this chapter, it's obvious that this quandary is universal, yet for each of us a unique and personal challenge. Thankfully, some of us have recognized that attending to our personal needs emotionally and physically is not, as some might say, selfish. It's simple self-preservation. Others are not quite there, lashing out at husbands who are the only ones getting "me time" (and punishing them with cold water in the shower!) and standing on the sidelines wondering how and when to find time for a shower themselves.

Many of the mothers who share their secrets and stories here reveal that if anything, they are resourceful. Yes, they are strapped for time, but a primal need to have some of it to themselves has led them to seek it out in the least likely ways and in the least likely places. For one mom, giving blood became even more than a philanthropic gesture—it was an hour of R & R, complete with someone serving her juice and cookies for a change. I, too, confess to this "donating blood as me time" trend, but I have taken it one step further. I recognized that by giving the more coveted commodity of platelets, the one hour of time to myself could become two hours of excused absence, with not only cookies, but computer access, too.

As mothers, the grand evolutionary design forces laser focus and deep commitment to our young charges. But what good are we to anyone if we do this at the cost of our own well-being? Easier said than done for most of us, I know. But not impossible.

For me, it's the often-heard words of a flight attendant that keep me on the straight and narrow. "If you are traveling with young children, fasten your own oxygen mask first." So simple and so true. At 35,000 feet, or more likely on the ground, if we can breathe easily, we're a whole lot better equipped to keep everyone else safe and sound.

Somewhere along the way I lost myself. I got so tied up being his wife and being their mom I forgot who I was in all this. Several months ago I decided it is okay to put myself first sometimes. I will put on my makeup just because, I will go to the gym just because, and I will buy myself something once in a while even if it is a splurge just because! One of my older kids noticed and asked me who I was meeting. I think I kind of worried him for a minute; he thought I might be stepping out on my husband, which I would never do since I am more loyal than Rover! I even buy myself roses sometimes just because! It makes a difference—just go ahead and give it a try!

I flush the toilet (in the guest bathroom) when my husband is taking a shower because I resent the fact that he actually gets any time alone without the kids bothering him. I know he gets a shot of cold water because he screams. I smile.

I'm sick of the fact that every conversation I have with my friend is really a competition to see who has the smarter kid.

I just e-mailed Nick Jr. to complain that they started advertising the new Backyardigans show too early, since my kids don't have a concept of time. Is this really my life? I'm more concerned about kids programming than national news?

Putting my baby in childcare a couple days a week, working full-time (three days at home and two in the office), and getting babysitters every couple of weeks so I can have a social life makes me a better mother. Having a self separate from my daughter makes me cherish and enjoy every second I spend with her and keeps my marriage healthy and happy. I don't have to feign happiness because I chose to be a SAHM. Having more to my individuality than being just a wife and mother makes me better at both those jobs, and my child and husband thank me for it.

To get alone time in my house, I tell my husband I have to poop, when I really don't. I shut and lock the door, and play a few rounds of hand-held Yahtzee.

I've forgotten what it feels like to be groped by hands that aren't sticky.

Where do these moms find the time and the money to go shopping and have "retail therapy"? I am lucky if I remember to buy a new pack of socks at the grocery store!

All I ask for is forty-five minutes in the morning. Two cups of coffee and a chance to look at the newspaper. How can you have so much damn energy already?? Crap. I HATE mornings.

THERE IS NO "I" IN MOMMY

As a teenager I used to yell at my mom for getting so involved in my life and for giving up stuff she wanted so she could give me what I wanted. Now I have a child and I can see why she wanted to and did give up so much for our happiness. Great mothers do that. I hope I don't give up as much as she did but I appreciate her so much more now. Nothing makes you appreciate your mother like becoming one.

I can't wait to wean my daughter so I can get stoned again.

THERE IS NO "I" IN MOMMY

I watch Cinemax After Dark on Demand for a little "me time" while my toddler naps in the afternoon.

I used to dread getting gas. But now I enjoy it 'cause I just stand there getting a couple minutes of "me time." Sounds pathetic, I know. I must need a vacation!

My "me time" is this: strap the kids in their car seats, drive through Starbucks, drive around town while the kids sleep, look at big magnificent houses and dream of the day I might live in one. Sigh.

I let my kid watch television so I can have "me time" and read/write blogs.

THERE IS NO "I" IN MOMMY

I wish someone had told me . . .

I wish someone had told me that I was an alcoholic and that there was a solution.

I wish someone had told me not to get a tattoo!

I wish someone had told me not to marry my best friend. It isn't for everyone. I love my husband, but there is NO passion. NONE. EVER. He's a great guy, but I just wish we weren't always buddies, and we could just be passionate lovers, once in a while.

I wish someone had told me that when you turn forty you realize you feel no guilt or shame or regret over anything you did when you were younger. SOOOO liberating.

I wish someone had told me that the only thing I needed to cure the insomnia I had throughout my twenties was a child!

"This medicine is going to work *really* fast."

by Liz Gumbinner

"I need some medicine, Mommy," Thalia insists, rubbing her eyes and dragging her slippered feet across the kitchen floor.

I head to the bathroom medicine cabinet holding a sippy cup half full of milk. I turn my back to the two-and-a-half-year-old standing in the doorway, and make a big dramatic show of lifting off the lid, adding something unseen to it, then giving it a good shake before I hand her the cup, gently guiding her toward her bedroom.

"Now let's go lie down now. This medicine is going to work *really* fast."

And she agrees.

My little Judy Garland.

I'm not entirely sure when the old sleeping-medicine

trick came about. I do remember Thalia had a cold, and after a few nights of cherry-flavored cough syrup before bed, she insisted on it. Nate pretended to put some in her milk. I tsked him. "This is a terrible idea!" I said. "She's not supposed to like medicine! She's going to grow up a hypochondriac! She's going to end up the first ever three-year-old drug addict sniffing paper cement in her preschool class!" But slowly, slowly I gave in.

Sometimes we choose short-term benefits over long-term solutions. One little white lie turning into more little white lies—every night. For weeks.

She closes her eyes and breathes deeply, like she's waiting for the drugs to kick in. At last she drifts off. I hate myself.

And yet, I kind of don't miss the bedtime battles one bit.

Liz Gumbinner tells two truths and a lie at www.mom-101 .blogspot.com

Things I Can't Say

"I wish my son were as smart as other kids."

I've been pretty confessional throughout this book, happy to fess up to my personal flaws and foibles. I've put my life under the microscope for the greater good of motherhood—so moms don't have to waste another second of their precious time wondering, "Am I normal?" But when asked to sign my name to my deepest, darkest thoughts, the ones I find even hard to admit having, let alone saying out loud, I need to draw the line. While I believe that bad thoughts don't connote bad mother, I'm not sure my kids, husband or friends would agree if they could hear the little voices in my head.

I *will* share this: almost weekly I contribute some doozies to the confessional, many of them echoing sentiments shared in this chapter ranging from regret to remorse, from anger to fear and loathing. I've had some very un-PC thoughts regarding my maternal love, my wifely duties and yes, my fellow PTA members. While I'm not taking ownership of mine, I'm grateful that under the veil of anonymity, so many moms have shared theirs and joined in this most candid of conversations. They've broached topics considered taboo in the corners of the playground or the playgroup—that they have a favorite child, that they were disappointed when an ultrasound picture revealed a boy (and they'd obviously longed for a girl), that they can't stand their friends' kids and that sometimes they can't stand their own.

I wish I'd known that thoughts of jumping in my car in the dead of night to leave my screaming three-week-old with her father and the dog was not a sign of mental illness but rather quite common for those of us subjected to raging hormones and sleep-deprivation. It would have saved me a lot of self-doubt and time spent on the therapist's couch.

Some days (like today) my favorite member of the household is the cat.

THINGS I CAN'T SAY

My son is six months old and I still don't trust my husband with him alone for more than an hour.

I left an intellectually stimulating job to stay at home with my kids. Most days all I do is change diapers and cater to their constant demands. Every day I wonder if the sacrifice I made is worth it.

I sometimes fantasize about getting divorced just so I could have every other weekend off.

My husband is a better parent then I am. He cooks, he plays with them more, he's more patient. I know that if I died young they would all grow up fine without me. I love and hate him for that.

THINGS I CAN'T SAY

I'm going to be really disappointed if the ultrasound shows that this baby is a boy. I have two boys and I love them so much, but I REALLY want a girl . . .

I secretly wish my three-year-old would just pee in the pool. Having to run him into the bathroom, pull down his wet trunks and wait while he "tries" three times every hour just gets old!

THINGS I CAN'T SAY

The real reason we can't go to play at your friend's house is because the mommies don't play well together.

I couldn't wait until the day my children said the word "Mommy." Now I just wish they would stop.

THINGS I CAN'T SAY

I hate my mother-in-law. I pretend that I've forgiven her for the horrible things she's said and done, but deep down I know I'll never really forgive her.

I HATE Elmo. I wish Big Bird would peck him to death.

189

Whenever my husband is really late coming home, I wonder if he's been in an accident and then I think about all the things I could do with his life insurance money. That's usually when I hear his key in the door and I feel both guilty and slightly disappointed at the same time.

I'm not sure my husband really loves his children. I'm not sure he really loves me. I love him so much though.

THINGS I CAN'T SAY

My DH and I had an eighteen-month-old and decided that we would try for number two. Much to our surprise, we got pregnant right away. At eight weeks, I had a miscarriage. I was grateful. At the time I was not ready to start on the road to motherhood again. Now, we have a four-year-old and a one-year-old. The two are a perfect pair and I feel that the loss was meant to be. I have never told a soul that I was glad to have miscarried.

Money may not buy happiness, but it certainly buys OPTIONS.

I wish my son were as smart as other kids.

DH's weight is turning me off. He knows he's fat, but he doesn't know he's getting a lot less booty because his body makes me sad. I'm too chicken to say anything.

THINGS I CAN'T SAY

I had a horrible day with my four-month-old son. Why did I decide to have a baby?? I can't remember any-more...Oh that's right, DH wanted one. And he's at work all day and won't soothe, bathe, or otherwise look after his son. *Grrrrrrr.*

I used to think women who got upset over not having a child of a certain gender were kind of dumb. Then I found out I am having another boy and now you can call me the biggest hypocrite in the world. Don't get me wrong; I'll love and cherish this baby and would just die if anything went wrong from here on out. But we are done at two, so I feel like I am mourning the loss of dresses and ribbons and seeing my husband with a Daddy's little girl. Is it OK to be happy to have a healthy beautiful boy inside me, yet cry for what I'll never have?

I never thought I'd say . . .

**"If you are going to kill each other,
go outside and do it!!"**

"No, you can't have a Band-Aid
on your tongue."

"Please don't eat your boogers."

"Noooo! Get your face out of the toilet!"

"Can you just lay off the arts and crafts
for a while and watch TV? At least
that isn't messy!"

True Mom Poll
Do you feel like you settled when you got married?

No. Not at all. Married my true love: **48%**

Yes. Definitely. Wanted kids and security
so I married him: 8%

Yes. Mr. Right got away so I married this one: 12%

None of the above. It's more complicated
than that 32%

"Tomorrow, in fact, might not be another day."

by Kara Swisher

"Look at me, Mom."

I hate to admit it, but I didn't look. On average, like most four-year-olds, Louie's look-at-me requests come in at a rate of three a minute these days. I know I am a bad mother for doing this (and, worse, admitting it!), but increasingly I don't actually look and then mumble a "Looking good," or "Cool" to assuage his need for my riveted attention.

"But, Mom," he pressed one night last week. "Looooook. I'm sixteen." That line jerked my head up immediately, and when I did look at him I saw he was standing tall atop the kitchen chair, hands on his hips, thrusting his small chin upward and shaking his dirty blond mane. "I am sixteen and almost an adult," he declared. And so he was, hugely proud of his most excellent performance as the doubt-lessly lanky teen that he would someday become. In fact, it was such a good glimpse forward that it almost made me cry, because I could envision him standing there a dozen years hence, his gangly youth and incipient adult-hood clashing for supremacy.

The near tears were actually not because I am senti-mental, because I am not, but for much more practical reasons: I never thought I could imagine such a future happening. That is no small thing, because until I had kids, I had never been able to have any clear picture of the future at all. You see, my father died when I was only five years old and that was the moment when I learned a cruel lesson that tomorrow, in fact, might not be another day.

He was only thirty-four years old. Dr. Louis Bush Swisher died from the complications of a brain aneurysm that burst without warning one sunny Sunday morning less than forty years ago. I watched as my brother knocked purposefully on the door of my parents' bedroom to get my father up. It was locked, and Jeffrey turned the knob round and round and hit the door with his hip.

We both thought my father had fallen into a deep sleep in there while writing a speech he was to give the next day. So Jeff kept kicking the door and smacking it and making such a noise that my mother finally came up, knocked impatiently and said, "Bush, Bush, open up the door right now; you're making Jeff very upset." But he did not wake.

After that, it was quick: the firemen coming to axe the door to splinters, the ambulance and stretcher with all sorts of things hanging off it. And the extraordinary silence when it was over.

Inevitably, my father would come up often. Meeting new people, there would always be the question: "What does your dad do?"

"Nothing," I'd always reply. "He died."

"Oh, I am so sorry," went the stock response. I always felt bad because I wanted to explain that it was okay, and anyway it was a long time ago and I was doing fine. But all I would see was an embarrassed face, a definite conversation stopper.

I could make up hours from the minutes of such moments. And others: empty Father's Days; an absent parent at school plays; good grades without his pat on the back; a prom with no lectures on being safe. And what else was missed? The love, I suppose, most of all.

What stayed for good was the stark definition such a tragic and drastic event gave to my whole life, in ways so inevitable and so clichéd. I am great in a crisis (don't panic, people!) and not so great at forming attachments (anyone can die at any moment, don't you know?). Such an attitude, while jaunty, does lack the human touch.

And this is in part why, from a very early age, I decided I wanted very much to have children, from whom you can never, either emotionally or physically, escape. I don't mean to sound like a touchy-feely California type here, but I knew that I could finally get over the death of my father only by having kids of my own. How to do this, given I had been gay for as long as I remember, though, would prove to be a journey I could never have imagined, especially since imagining the future had never been my strong suit.

As I was thinking back on the particulars of having Louie and later his brother, Alex, on the night of his impromptu teen show, Louie seemed to be reading my mind in a most alarming way. "I'm not really sixteen yet, Mom," he said. "That wasn't real."

"I know, sweetie, that's a long time away," I answered distractedly.

"Actually," he declared, "I wish I could stay four forever and you would never die, even when you get old."

Me, too, I thought. Me, too.

Kara Swisher is a technology columnist and founder of the *Wall Street Journal*'s website Allthingsd.com

Sexy Mamas

"It wasn't with my husband."

Over an after-school snack, my then eleven-year-old daughter, Phoebe, sat with two of her girlfriends, whispering conspiratorially. The rumor de jour was that several older girls had been caught giving BJs in the bathroom at school. Trained to ask what was known—or more importantly what was thought to be known—before offering up an opinion or information, I asked casually, "Do you guys even know what a BJ is?"

"Duh. Of course we do!" they snapped. I seized this learning opportunity and launched into the importance of self-respect and loving relationships. Just as I was about to throw in the "Oral sex IS sex . . . I don't care what Clinton says," Phoebe interrupted me and asked, "Do you do that with Tom (my husband, her stepdad)?"

"Well, uh, yes." I stammered. (Although as Tom is reading this he is definitely shaking his head and thinking, "Not nearly enough.")

"And did you do that with my dad?"

"Well, uh, yes." (Ditto here for Jeremy, my ex . . . he's agreeing with Tom.)

Before the inquisition could go any further, I laid down the ground rules—I would talk about anything but refused to be the star of any sexual scenario discussed. No exceptions.

Sex—talking about it and certainly how we think and feel about it—is a favorite topic among mothers in the confessional. Like me, moms share embarrassing stories of their tweens and teens recognizing and then recoiling from any evidence of their parents' sexuality. They share tales of unrequited longing ("I want it every night—why doesn't he?"), of lack of desire ("I left my libido in the delivery room") and assorted tales of trying to find the time and the place to get in touch with their inner seductress while wiping sticky faces, juggling work and driving carpool. The Madonna-whore complex carries on with a vengeance and while there are no answers—perhaps only more questions—it's at least comforting to know that it's a constant struggle for all of us to get to that place of lust, longing and wild sexual abandon with the creatures we created out of all this in the first place just a few feet away.

Sometimes when my husband and I are in a fight, I purposely wear sexy underwear just to rub it in that he won't be getting any that night.

I left my three kids in our hotel room in New York and had sex with my husband in the stairwell.

My niece calls having sex "baking cookies." My husband and I call it "going camping" because he brings the tent!

I couldn't care less if I never had sex with my husband again. I have my vibrators. They make me happy and don't leave the toilet seat up.

We just found out our friends are swingers. I won't admit it to DH, but I'm slightly interested.

SEXY MAMAS

Why are there still dishes in the sink? Because Mommy needed a time-out with her vibrator. That's why.

I constantly fantasize about leaving my husband . . . for a woman.

I think about my ex constantly; I want to hook up with him one last time.

I just realized that I actually considered cheating with the dad of my kid's classmate. Thing is, I'm not attracted to him in the least; I just know that he is attracted to me, and that makes me feel good about myself. What is wrong with me?

I've always wanted to be ravished, pushed down to the bed and have my clothes ripped off. I just didn't imagine it would come in the form of a tantrum-wielding toddler, impatient for boobs.

I put on a baby DVD and plopped my son in front of the television so I could have sex. It wasn't with my husband.

I'm a SAHM and my husband gives me money to give him BJ's. That's the only money I get to spend on myself.

I wish my husband would hold me like he used to before we had kids.

I'm a put-together woman who works, has a great house and family. My husband is perfect and truly loves me. I'm a poster-perfect mother who doesn't do anything out of the norm. But when I see a punk with tattoos down both arms and a mohawk, I want to run away with him.

My husband is deployed and today I had a massage . . . by a MAN, which I requested. I am so freaking horny. He rubbed me all over including my ass and I could hardly relax at all. He kept asking if I was OK, and I said, "Yes, just a little jumpy!" God, I am desperate for some lovin'. Hurry up, husband, and get home!

I have a fantasy that a really hot stripper would pay me a visit (when I have no kids around! Yeah right!). The part that would be a major turn-on is when he got to his thong, he wouldn't stuff his junk in my face, he would whip out cleaning supplies. He would dance around as he deep-cleaned my house, windows, grout, the fridge. That would get me off! Come to think of it he wouldn't even need to be hot, so long as he cleaned well.

I know that the husband of a good friend of mine from playgroup is cheating on her. I feel terrible, but I think he deserves to cheat because his wife neglects him and always tells us how she refuses to have sex with him.

SEXY MAMAS

When my husband got home tonight, I was so tired of being "Mama! Mama! Mama!" that I sat the kids down to watch SpongeBob, locked the bathroom door and let DH have his way with me. . . . It was a selfish, emotional break, but damn, it felt good and now he's at the playground with our kids. Life is good.

I still feel kind of hot driving my minivan.

I gave my children a wonderful Xmas last year . . . using the money I'd made as an escort.

I look people in the eye hoping that I'll be someone's missed connection on craigslist.

When I don't feel like having sex, I pretend that I have no choice, he owns me and can do whatever he wants. That gets me into the mood—fast. Fantasies are hot.

I have a massive crush on a lesser known British actor named Andrew Knott. When I am having sex with my husband, I pretend it's him.

229

I pretend that I shop at Whole Foods because feeding organic food to my family is important, but mostly I just shop there to ogle the tattooed, crunchy, earthy guys.

I am the other woman AND the wife. I feel like a hypocrite.

I love my DH and don't want anyone else, but I have a major crush on my OB-GYN doctor.

Once again I just found porn on our computer. I'm livid. Why do men need to see this all the time? I'm a woman who loves sex. I could see if I didn't, but I do. They just don't get how hurtful it is to be made to feel like you're just not good enough, which is what porn does. It's just another way for men to send the message that this is what you should look like, this is how you should act. Respect us for being good wives and mothers? No. But let some slut spread her legs for the world to see, and she's just amazing.

I should be taking Zoloft. I went off it because of the side effects: low libido and weight gain. Now I'm super anxious all the time and I have to decide if I want to be skinny, horny, and on the verge of a mental breakdown or chubby, unorgasmic, but emotionally stable. Swimsuit season is just around the corner...decisions, decisions.

When I play with my kids and dance with them, I tend to get horny for my husband.

SEXY MAMAS

I'm five months pregnant and have only gained 10 pounds! I think I look amazing! I certainly FEEL sexier than I ever have in my life, but my husband won't lay a finger on me. He says that me having a baby in me makes him "feel weird" about having sex. I'm horny as hell!! What do I do? HELP!!!

I wish someone had told me . . .

I wish someone had told me that it's OK to grow to love your baby. I thought something was wrong with me because I did not "instantly melt with overwhelming love for her the second she was born." Now that she's a few weeks old I do love her more than anything.

I wish someone had told me that no matter how successful you are, no matter how intelligent, no matter how much you have achieved, your husband will still expect you to wash the dishes, do the laundry and take care of the kids because you're a woman.

I wish someone had told me that nothing would be the same after I had children. Nothing. I don't even watch the news in the same way.

I wish someone had told me that life isn't about the end result; it's about the journey that gets you there. Don't rush to the finish line. Take it slow, and enjoy the ride. It's not what you've done that makes you who you are; it's what you take from it. Live, love and never stop learning.

"My children make me feel very weak."

by Erin Kotecki Vest

Today my firstborn son turned five.

We did the cake. We did the presents. We did the hoopla.

He was beaming all day and I was making a huge deal out of his ability to have accomplished five years of living.

Inside I was dying.

I spent the day in fear. I spent the day in denial. I put on a happy face but inside I was in PAIN because of his big boy bike. His wanting to shut the door when he went to the bathroom. His growing up.

It hurts. I'm not a fan. And I'd like it to stop.

The entire time I was encouraging him to sit on the new bike and test it out and he was protesting that it looked too big and was too wobbly, I was thinking, "It's OK, baby boy. Don't be afraid, Mom is here, don't do it if you don't want to, just come sit on my lap and lay your head on my shoulder and cuddle with me."

I stood there thinking to myself, if you can't handle the wobbly big kid bike, I can't possibly let you out there into the world and let you see how horrible things are, how your heart will be broken, how people will be mean, how sometimes your stomach will be in knots, how life can be very shitty . . .

I was sick. SICK.

My children make me feel very weak. The kind of weak that could turn me into some insane helicopter mom who homeschools and layers the walls with foam. The kind of weak that makes me throw every ounce of common sense out the window in favor of whatever will keep my children in ignorant bliss for eternity.

It hurts too much. IT HURTS TOO MUCH.

Of course I gently coaxed him onto that bike and eventually he was riding around the cul-de-sac and life was just happy-happy but I couldn't shake the amount of fear that came with this birthday.

Real school is around the corner. Big kids who bully. Teachers who may or may not find his quirks endearing. Expectations. Disappointments. Triumphs.

I ache for every moment yet to come that causes him to

pause. I yearn for every moment passed that seems now to have been so much easier. I want nothing more than to stop time and pretend as though none of this is happening.

I feel like a failure of a mother for entertaining these thoughts and trying to will them into reality. Like if I blink hard enough I can *poof* us all back to when my biggest fear was him hitting his head while learning to walk.

I'm not good at this. I'm just not. I spend most of my day trying to keep my children busy so I can ignore them and the other half complaining as I deal with them. Then I have the gall to be upset at the passing of time and the reality of children becoming adults. These small creatures bring out every weakness I have and throw it on the table for all to see, dripping in emotion and exposing what is best, but mostly what is the worst, inside my soul.

Tonight I watched my five-year-old glow as he blew out five candles. I watched his little sister, eyes as big as saucers, ready and willing to take her turn at the cake in six days when she turns three. As I discreetly exhaled to help extinguish the flames, I wished right along with my baby boy.

Keep him safe. Make this hurt less. Make me strong.

Happy Birthday.

Erin Kotecki Vest reigns at queenofspainblog.com

Making It Work

"You're perfect because you're not perfect."

Yesterday I forgot to attend my son's violin recital at school. The event was clear as day in my calendar but somehow it didn't make it onto my *to-do* list for the day. And for me—if it's not on the list, it might as well not be happening. So when my son called me from Grandma's car after school and wailed, "Mom, why weren't you there?" I was stunned. That numb feeling quickly morphed into shock and then sadness—for my son and for me. I felt my face go hot and red and while sitting in front of my colleague, the tears fell like a leaky faucet and I thought to myself: this is it; this is the event that's going to plant him on the shrink's couch struggling to get to the root of his abandonment issues.

I responded honestly—perhaps too honestly, my voice

cracking, "Oh. My. God. I am so sorry, Owen. I forgot. I don't know how I could have. But I forgot."

"You always forget," he said.

"No, I don't," I stammered. "You know that's not true. I am sooooo sorry."

We met at the park just a few minutes later and I ran across the baseball field to where he was warming up for his Little League game. I knelt down to eye level and still weepy, said my most sincere apology. My emotions confused him and he wriggled away from me.

"It's OK, Mom. Really. It's OK."

But it didn't feel OK. I can forget a snack. Or a sweater. Or a teacher's birthday. But the image of my little man with his violin perched on his shoulder, squeaking out "Twinkle Twinkle Little Star" while scanning the room for his mom just about killed me.

To make matters worse, that night Owen woke up with a night terror. He's suffered from these odd, spooky nightmares for years—the ones where despite my holding him tight, he screams, "Mommmy!!! Help me! I need my mommy!!!"

The tears fell again and I sat in silence rocking him, whispering in his ear and hoping he might hear me, "It's OK baby. Mommy's here. Mommy is so sorry. Mommy will do better tomorrow."

Motherhood is humbling to say the least. It challenges

us to be our best and forces us to accept our worst. Despite our good intentions to NOT do as was done to us, we seasoned veterans know that even if we break one generational cycle, we're destined to create a new one. At all costs, we might become sticklers for punctuality (because Mom was always late to pick us up from school), but then we become the mom who forgets to give her kids money for the *one day* there's a bake sale at school or worse, the mom who doesn't read the small print on the birthday invitation and sends her child dressed as a civilian into a sea of swashbuckling, pint-sized pirates.

Our offenses may run the gamut but our remorse and guilt and slow road to self-acceptance are universal. Thankfully our children seem to forgive (and forget?) faster than we do ourselves, and our friends are always on hand to offer reassurance and confessions of offenses far worse than our own.

I, after two years, finally feel like I can do a pretty good job as a mom. Not a great job, but I'm really beginning to come into my own as a mother. It's great. Sad that it took so long, but great.

When I was pregnant I told a friend I hoped I was having a boy because I didn't want to share my husband with another female. Since my baby girl arrived I love her more and more each day. I actually think my husband is the one who feels left out! No one could have prepared me for how much love I feel for my daughter. She's the most wonderful thing ever. I hope these feelings I have for her never change, but I know our relationship with each other will only get more complicated as she grows older. I cherish every moment of this blissful time when she's young and innocent.

MAKING IT WORK

I love being a single mom. I don't think I would know how to love a man and my baby fairly at the same time.

There are days that I just don't care that their toys are sprawled over every square inch of available floor space or that their clothes don't match or that they aren't wearing socks with their shoes. I just don't care as long as they are happy, healthy and whole.

I spent my whole life being jealous of, resenting and generally disliking other women. Since I've been a mom, I've found out I really like women's friendship. They're fun and wise and enrich my life.

TRUE MOM CONFESSIONS

Tucking my son in last night I apologized for losing my temper that morning. He looked up at me and said, "Don't worry, Mommy, you're perfect. You're perfect because you're not perfect." What a special boy. What a lucky mom.

I just got a brand-new breast pump and I love it. Like I used to love a sexy pair of new shoes. I am such a mom.

Today I decided I would try to do things a little differently. I listened more carefully when my kids were talking. I tore myself away from the computer and helped them—really helped them with their homework. I told my husband I loved him. It was a good day.

Before my son's birth I bought one of those cook-books and a top-of-the-line food processor so I could make all his baby food myself, using all organic and whole grain ingredients. He's almost one year old and I haven't made one thing with it. Instead I buy low-sodium soup and strain out the broth and wash off all the ingredients (too salty) and dump it on his high chair. It's nice and mushy and this way he's eating his veggies and beans, etc. Why did I think the process of giving birth would turn me into a wonderful chef? For that matter, why did I think giving birth would make me a perfect person?

I love living what some people consider a mediocre life. I am a minivan-driving, Starbucks-drinking, fake-boob-having suburbanite and I wouldn't have it any other way.

I kiss twenty little toes, twenty little fingers, four little eyes, two little noses, four little ears, two little bellies and two sweet little mouths before bed each night. Sometimes, our time-consuming bedtime routine seems a little over-the-top, but I wouldn't change it for the world. I love my munchkins!

I was Supermom yesterday. Worked, took care of baby, cooked, gave DH great sex. Today, I'm exhausted, so there will be no "Wednesday" Supermom.

MAKING IT WORK

I am determined to have a good day today and be proud of the person and mom that I am. Sometimes I feel this is just a choice.

My daughter will be one in April and I realized this morning . . . she's a pretty cool kid. She yelled at her dad this morning for me when he wouldn't answer me when I called for him!! Go, baby girl! Who loves Mama?!

I love my husband! I love my kids! I love my life! So bills sometimes pile up, and we can't go on trips or vacations or have that big house! So what?! I would rather be at home in our small house spending quality time with my kids, volunteering in their schools and making meals for the family than live in a big beautiful home, and be too busy working to do all the things I love to do for my family!

I have found the man of my dreams. He just happens to be fat, bald and four weeks old.

MAKING IT WORK

When my daughter was a newborn, an older cousin asked, "Do you ever just sit there and hold her while she's sleeping and just watch her? All day?" I sheepishly answered yes. She said, "It's okay, you know. To just sit and watch them. I did it all the time. My house still hasn't resumed complete order and there are still dishes in the sink." Her daughter was eleven at the time. It was probably the best advice I got. Now my daughter is two and sometimes I still just watch her. When she's sleeping or playing or running outside, I just stop. And watch. There are still dishes in my sink, too.

I never thought I'd say . . .

**"No, those are Mommy's tampons.
They are not Christmas tree
ornaments."**

"No, honey, people aren't hatched.
They come out of the potty place!"

"STOP licking the road salt off
the side of the van!"

"I want another baby."

True Mom Poll
Do you ever wonder "what if" about men in your past?

Yes, often: 38%

Yes, but only on a really bad day with my
husband! 19%

Nope. Never. I'm with my true love: 32%

Nope. But now that you bring it up . . . there
was this one guy 4%

None of the above: 6%

"I never stopped checking, checking, checking."

by Connie Schultz

It was a new stage in life for both of us—she had just turned seven; I had just turned into a single mother—when my daughter stood in the middle of the empty apartment and predicted our future.

"Mommy," she said, grinning, "I think we're going to be really happy here."

I swallowed hard and smiled.

"Yeah?" I said.

"Oh, yeah," she said, nodding. "I can just feel it."

That was fourteen years ago, the beginning of a time when I would spend months—make that years—in shallow breathing, pacing the floors at night like a ghost in my own home.

What, I wondered, would happen to my little girl?

I worried about money, of course, starting with how I was going to furnish an entire apartment. Basically, all I took with us were a few boxes of clothes, most of our family photos and all of my books. Oh, and the Christmas decorations—an odd thing to pack at the height of a personal crisis, perhaps, but I'd spent more than a decade hand-stitching dozens of ornaments. Beyond their sentimental value, which was considerable, they offered the only hard evidence I had that I really did try to make it as the homemaker my then-husband had always wanted. I found out just how committed he was to that notion of marital bliss only after I took my first full-time job. Three months after my first day at the newspaper, he filed for divorce.

"If you quit your job, we can call this off," he said.

Eleven years of a hard marriage were over.

My worries about money were nothing compared to my fears for my daughter. My story is as old as that of the first single mother. My every conscious move, my every comment, was meant to assure Caitlin that I was the grown-up and she had nothing to worry about. The only things missing from my Super Mommy routine were tights, a cape and a snappy soundtrack. I coached her softball team, skipped lunches for almost a year to buy her a used upright piano and made dolls from scratch, stitching a red heart on each of their chests around the words, "Mommy loves Caitlin."

All the while, I never stopped checking, checking, checking for signs that I was ruining her forever.

Every nightmare, every temper tantrum, every tearful plea for attention I examined for signs of bad mothering. No matter what else was going on in her life, I was certain that her every step was more labored because of the invisible burden I, her mother, for God's sake, had forced onto her narrow little shoulders.

So. The years passed. Caitlin went to the prom and graduated from high school and left for college just like all of her classmates from two-parent homes. I remarried, and she loves my husband. And me. Still, me. Wow.

We are a sentimental family, and our home is full of framed photos and childhood art. When all of our kids are home, or friends come for dinner, likely as not Caitlin is the one to bring up a childhood memory. So often, she will turn to me and say, "Mom, remember when . . ." Almost always, she is pulling up a memory from our time together in that apartment, when she was just a little girl and I was a mother full of promises.

Every time, she smiles as she talks. "We were so happy there," she always says.

And every time, I smile, too, relieved by her happy memory.

But secretly, I am always checking, checking, checking.

Because some fears just never go away.

Connie Schultz is a Pulitzer Prize–winning journalist, author and columnist for the *Cleveland Plain Dealer*.